BeakSpeak:

A Fable and Language Workbook

Peggy Marceaux

© Copyright © 2019 BeakSpeak by Peggy Marceaux

All rights reserved. No part of this book may be reproduced or transmitted in any form or by any means, electronic or mechanical, including photocopying, recording, or by any information storage or retrieval system, without permission in writing from the publisher.

ISBN: 978-1-941345-30-6 HB
ISBN: 978-0-463776-69-8 SW
ASIN: B07Q33GPQV

Erin Go Bragh Publishing
Canyon Lake, TX

Manufactured in the United States of America
Printed and Bound by Ingram
Book Design by Kathleen's Graphics
The text of the book is Amarante & Comic Sans MS
Illustrations by Mike Forshay
Original Character Designs by Debbie Marceaux in 2009

Download printable worksheets for classrooms at:
www.ErinGoBraghPublishing.com/books/beakspeak

Acknowledgements:

I would like to say a special thank you to my wonderful sister-in-law, Debbie Marceaux, for creating the template for our characters. Her vision helped our illustrator bring these characters to life. There has never been one thing I've ever asked of Debbie that she hasn't found some way to deliver, even while caring for a family and holding down a full-time job. The character template is just such an example.

As well, I'd like to thank friends and teachers, Ann Farmer and Danettte Bermea, for giving of their time and skills to edit the manuscript. I would be remiss, of course, not to thank my "partner-in-crime," Jo Beth McElrath, who always provides emotional, and oftentimes financial, support. Finally, I must give the bulk of my appreciation to my publisher Kathleen Shields, whose guidance, encouragement and expertise has enabled this little book to take shape and breathe. She has been a godsend, an inspiration and a joy with whom to work.

This little book has been a dream of mine since I started raising and loving chickens some thirty years ago. When I had to give them up, I felt realizing this book would allow me to immortalize some of the personalities in my last flock – and yes, chickens **DO** have personalities, just like dogs and cats. Plus, as a retired English teacher, I felt I still had something to teach young people about thinking and language skills. I am so humbled this little piece of me has come to fruition.

The original **BeakSpeak** Characters hand drawn by Debbie Marceaux © 2009

How did BeakSpeak come about?

My first experience with "fowl" language started many years ago when I met an old codger named T. Brady who introduced me to his game flock. A reincarnation of Dale Gribble from the animated sitcom, *King of the Hill*, T. would mumble and cluck when he talked to them, which I found surprisingly soothing.

That Barnyard Zen belied the fact that chickens have a rough life: they must survive a pecking order. Yes, though a flock of chickens may be a microcosm of human society, some behaving aggressively, others passively, weak birds cannot survive a bully without a human intervening.

I could see myself doing that. So, I bought some chickens, but that's another story. I mostly wanted to help young *people* survive bullying. I wanted to help them become independent-minded, too, and to get along with one another. To do that, you have to communicate what you mean to say.

My chicken coop, then, became the English classroom, where I taught language skills for 32 years in high school. My greatest reward was watching my students grow to respect one another, find their confidence, learn how to rationally think about the world around them, and then shape their views to fit in that world. I was able to help them do all this by teaching them that, when you think, speak and write precisely and concisely, using the clearest and most effective words, with the most energetic verbs to defend your views, the better you communicate your meaning.

You can learn to do this at *any* grade level. For instance, instead of saying my little fable, BeakSpeak, is about chickens who have trouble with communication, you say "the chickens communicate poorly because of learned, language errors" - or, when Nothing New Sue says "stop beating around the bush, Sean, you are red just like Henny Penny, and you *are* mad right now." Cut to the chase with "Stop stalling, Sean. You are both red like Henny Penny *and* mad right now." Of course you also need to expose general language errors, which I do by attaching young chickens to them who speak the examples.

Add to those techniques, stimulating thought with exploratory questions, which comes with my little book, and you have BeakSpeak. I even supply suggested answers.

I sorely regret having had to retire, but it eventually comes to all of us. I miss watching those young people blossom, but I merged my love for chickens and for language into BeakSpeak, hoping to create a different kind of classroom.

"I hope you find this book like fertile barnyard soil, designed to cultivate better language skills, clearer thinking, and loving kindness!"

BeakSpeak: A Fable and Language Workbook

The name <u>BeakSpeak</u> alludes* to *1984,* a novel by George Orwell, where countries are no longer able to speak or think freely in what they call the "Golden Country" of the past. They must learn a new language called "Newspeak", which does not allow people to say what they want or to challenge authority. <u>One reason why this little book is important</u> is because it helps its readers to avoid common errors in language that can hinder* clear communication and thinking processes.

<u>Another reason why this book is important</u> is because it is a fable, which is a story with animals as characters that deliver a moral*, or lesson. <u>Before reading BeakSpeak</u>, be sure to have read at least one of the older fables this book alludes to: either *Henny Penny, The Sky is Falling,* or *Chicken Little.*

<u>The characters</u> in **BeakSpeak** <u>include the teacher</u>, **Ms. Goldspeak**, whose name refers to Orwell's "Golden Country" in *1984.* She is an ideal example of good character and of someone who speaks eloquently*. She is a hen, an adult, female chicken, and is therefore of egg-laying age. Since she is a language teacher, she has no language problems. Other characters include:

* allude – refer to
* hinder – to keep from happening
* moral – lesson
* eloquent – language that clearly says what the speaker means

Three pullets, which are young female chickens who have not yet started to lay eggs. Their names, nicknames*, and language problems are listed below:

All-the-Same Jayne uses stereotypes (words that put people and ideas into categories).

Nothing-New Sue uses clichés (words and phrases said so many times over the years that they've become common).

Re-Say Renee uses redundancy (saying the same thing twice, though maybe using different words).

And four cockerels, which are young roosters. Their names, nicknames and language problems are listed below:

Short-Cut Sean uses texting shortcuts (clipped letters*, sometimes used with numbers, to say something as briefly as possible for texting).

Mixed-Up Chuck uses malapropisms (words mistakenly used for the right words that sound like them).

Fill-the-Space Chase uses empty words and sounds (that carry no meaning in the sentence at all).

Street-Talk Walt uses slang (informal, street language that replaces proper words).

---

* nicknames – pet names
* clipped letters – parts of word with some letters left out on purpose

Ms. Goldspeak's students entertain themselves in

Street-Talk Walt is a Production Red cockerel. He likes to impress others by acting "cool".

Mixed-Up Chuck is a Buff Orpington cockerel. He is large, plump, mild-mannered and friendly.

the chicken yard as they await the start of school.

Re-Say Renee is an Australorp pullet. She is large, black and easy going.

All-the-Same Jayne is a Barred Rock pullet. She is a large, prison-striped bird who is very aggressive*.

* aggressive – easily angered and likes to fight

Fill-the-Space Chase is a Bantam cockerel. He is small, multi-colored and very aggressive among others his size.

Nothing-New Sue is an Aracauna. She is average size whose color is an array* of earth tones. Her breed is so friendly the hens are often made house pets. They're called the Easter-egg chickens because they lay blue and green eggs.

* array — many different kinds

Short-Cut Sean is a Rhode Island Red cockerel. He is large and generally passive.

Ms. Goldspeak is a Brahma hen. She is large, wise and always calm.

BeakSpeak

In a little south-Texas chicken yard, a variety of pullets and cockerels are gathered about waiting for the Headrooster to announce the start of Ms. Goldspeak's English class. Sue, a smart little Aracauna with tufts of feathers puffed out under her ears, addressed the group. "Hey you clucks," she began, "let's play some kick ball until Mr. Chanticleer crows, and we have to toe-the-line again."

"Only if I can roll the ball for both teams," insisted Renee, a bright green sheen* reflecting in the sunlight off of her deep black feathers. "Australorps like me are good at doing one job really well, because we are so good at it," she repeated.

* sheen – shine

2

"Okay, Re-Say," mocked* Sue. "You can be the head-honcho pitcher if that's what floats your boat, but I'm picking my kickers." Sue turned to the others to select her team, when Walt, a red cockerel dressed in a sloppy tee shirt, stopped her short.

* mocked – made fun of

"Hold on Sue, he challenged. "You ain't picking first, Chick. My bros Chuck and Sean here will be kicking with **me**. You, Jayne and that little Banty* dude there can take the leftovers." While Walt and Chuck were laughing, Sean, a red Rhodie, looked up from his mobile phone at the mention of his name. *What did he say?* He thought for a moment, then just ignored everyone again and went back to playing with his phone.

"Hey! Who put **you** in charge, Walt?" Sue shouted. "What makes you think you're the top banana around here? You must have a loose screw or something. Well, I wouldn't be on your team if you begged me to be," Sue blubbered*, then huffed off to Jayne to be consoled.

* banty – by using this shortened form of Bantam, Walt is insulting Chase
* blubbered – partly pouted, partly cried

4

All-the-Same Jayne, however, wanted nothing to do with cowering* to bullies like Walt. The larger-than-average Barred Rock pullet became so angry her neck feathers puffed out, her wings spread wide, and her toes lifted her even higher than she normally stood. When Walt dared to laugh again, Jayne ran head long at him and knocked him down.

"Hey!" cried Chuck. "Leave him alone!" The usually mild-mannered Buff Orpington, large and slow, had to lumber* over to help Walt up. "You could have stilled him," he accused Jayne. "You hit him with so much source he may never be able to beak dance again," he sobbed, mixing up his words.

"Well, no matter what you say, Chuck, we are NOT letting him control who we want on our team," replied Jayne. "WE are picking who we want, not Walt. Right Renee?" Without waiting for Renee to agree, Jayne turned to face all six of the young chickens in the yard. "Now," she continued, "who wants to be on OUR side?"

* cowering – slink away fearfully
* lumber – to walk slowly because you are too large or heavy

"I do!" Sue declared, her wing waving wildly above her head.

Jayne sighed. "Of course you do. But who else?" Sue was heartbroken.

"Uh, like, nobody ever picks me," whispered the little bantam cockerel.

"What's that? Say what?" Jayne asked again, looking around for the chicken who spoke. Then Chase raised his tiny wing and replied, shyly, but a little louder this time. "Like, I'd like to, you know, be on your team, if you'll let me."

"Well, sure we'll let you, won't we, Renee? Now we have the team WE want," Jayne proudly proclaimed. "**You had nothing to say about it, Walt. It was all our own doing. So there!**"

Then, as Jayne, Renee, and Chase stepped over to Walt's side of the chicken yard to argue over which team would kick first, the Headrooster crowed.

And, so, school began. As the youngsters entered the room and took their seats that morning, a stately Light Brahma Hen walked into the classroom and faced her students. Walt was glad he didn't have to sit next to Jayne. "Good morning, Class," their teacher Ms. Goldspeak greeted, then reached for a familiar children's book on her desk. "Who can tell us something important we learned yesterday when we read *Henny Penny*?"

"I can, Ms. Goldspeak," crowed Street-Talk Walt, waving his wing proudly. When Ms. Goldspeak nodded his direction, the confident, red cockerel jumped to attention. "I remember learning that Henny Penny is a good egg," he said, and smiled broadly Jayne's direction.

Ms. Goldspeak put her wing tip to her beak. "Hmmm. Just what do you think Walt means when he says Henny Penny is a 'good egg'?" Ms. Goldspeak asked the class.

Walt looked surprised that his teacher didn't understand what he meant. Sensing a chance to get back at Walt for how he embarrassed* her in the yard, Nothing New Sue jumped to answer. "It means Henny Penny is nice all the time and never gets mean."

* embarrassed – made her feel ashamed

Impatient*, All-the-Same Jayne shook her head and blurted out, "I don't think so, Ms. Goldspeak." Before the teacher could turn toward the Barred Rock pullet, Jayne had added, "Because everybody knows that red chickens get mad all the time, and Henny Penny is red."

* Impatient – unable to wait

Ms. Goldspeak shook her head, clucked, and raised her wing to remind Jayne of the proper way to be recognized. Street-Talk Walt lowered his head. Although he wanted to defend himself, he didn't make a peep. He felt like Jayne was saying those things about *him*. After all, she was so rude to him in the chicken yard, and he was red just like the little hen in the story book.

Ms. Goldspeak smiled at Walt and slowly moved towards him. She put her wing gently on his shoulder. "Let's talk about that, Class. Is that true? Do you think chickens, who are red, get mad all the time?"

"Uh, yeh!" agreed Fill-the-Space Chase, the tiny, nervous Bantam. Ms. Goldspeak's nearness made him feel secure enough to speak his mind. She shook her head to remind him, too, to raise his wing. Chase had spoken out, though, because he felt he was so small he'd have to thrust his wing up as high as it would go and jump all around before Ms. Goldspeak would even notice him. When she finally did nod his way, he continued. "Like, remember," Chase beamed, "like, when Henny Penny squawked at the sky, like, as if *it* was the one, like, making all that stuff, uh, fall on top of her? She was *not* happy. She was, like, really upset."

Ms. Goldspeak squinted at Chase, as if she were trying to understand what he believed. "Does your word 'upset' mean angry, Chase? If not, what *does* it mean? Just what *is* Henny Penny truly feeling?"

Walt never looked up at his teacher. Her closeness to him and her questioning Chase gave Street-Talk Walt the courage to defend himself now. He frowned at Chase. "She's not angry," he dared.

Ms. Goldspeak's gaze met Chase's, but she quietly stepped back to her desk and let Walt defend himself.

"Henny Penny is getting a bad rap," Walt continued. "She wasn't mad. She was just really freaked, that's all." Walt didn't see Ms. Goldspeak knit her brows.

Instead of saying anything, though, the teacher decided to speak to Renee, whose frantic waving and jumping had turned over her desk.

"Okay, Renee," she said to Re-Say, "I'll get to you in just a moment. But first," she said to the little Bantam, "Chase, do you want to tell me what you meant by saying Henny Penny was upset, or do you want to respond to Walt?"

"Uh, I've got to, like, think about it some more, Ms. Goldspeak." Chase seemed confused and a little scared to challenge Walt.

His teacher was very pleased to hear one of her students wait and think things through before speaking, and she wanted Chase to overcome his natural fear of larger cockerels like Walt.

"Okay, Chase. Good for you," Ms. Goldspeak said, then turned Renee's way.

Once she heard her name called, Re-Say's eyes lit up. "Ms. Goldspeak, Henny Penny got *mad* at the sky, that's what she got. That's what I think. I don't think what Walt said is right." Walt slouched in his chair, crossed his arms and glared at Renee.

All-the-Same Jayne and Renee were best of friends, so it was no surprise that Jayne further expressed her bias* against Walt by smiling at Renee and adding, "Yes, I agree with Renee. All chickens get mad sometimes, but red chickens get mad *all* the time. I mean, even yellow chickens, who are always afraid, get mad sometimes."

* bias – to have something against someone for no good reason

Walt couldn't help but take what Jayne and Renee said to heart. He suddenly jumped up and started shouting at them, taking his teacher quite by surprise. "*I'm* red," he defended, "and I don't freak all the time! And what about Sean? He's a Rhodie like Henny Penny, so he's red, too, but he chills most of the time! I mean, no dude would chill if somebody was mean to him like you are to me. How would *you* feel if the sky roasted you like it did Henny Penny? That doesn't mean she's not cool at other times."

Walt looked at the cockerel at the end of the row. "Don't you think so, Sean?"

Short-Cut Sean was startled to hear his name. He had been busily texting a friend in another class instead of paying attention to what was going on. Sean quickly put his phone behind his back. "???" Sean thought, for he could not speak with his crooked beak.

    Ms. Goldspeak could tell that Sean was confused, so she had Walt repeat his point, but *calmly* this time, and to Sean rather than Jayne and Renee. Sean became upset. He shook his head, hurried up to the board and wrote "Ogr8! b4 ne1 thnx he noz my biz, plz m8k shr u get enuf fax!" then turned and glared at Walt.

Ms. Goldspeak looked him in the eyes. "Hand it to me, Sean." Forced to admit he broke the rules, Sean huffed and angrily handed her the phone.

That distraction was all a feisty* little Aracauna biddy* with fluffy, peach-colored face tufts needed to steal the class's attention away from the lesson.

She thrust both wings into the air and jumped up and down on her seat until her teacher looked her way and addressed Nothing-New Sue's exuberance*.

* feisty — spirited, spunky
* biddy — another name for pullet
* exuberance — full of energy

Walt broke in ahead of her, though. "Boy, who kicked you in the pants?"

"Walt." his teacher warned.

Sue, who considered herself the class clown, didn't pay Walt any mind. Her words were for Sean. "Stop beating around the bush, Sean," cackled Sue. "You are red just like Henny Penny, and you are mad right now. You were mad the other day, too, when I texted you that my dad said your dad was hen-pecked*. I thought you would try to scratch me with your tiny spurs* again like you did when I bet you your grandpa had ended up crispy-fried at Chicken Lickin'."

* hen-pecked – when a man (rooster) lets his wife (hen) tell him what to do
* spurs – curved, sharp, and hard growths that roosters have on the backs of their lower legs to protect themselves and their hens

21

Sue's words had most of the class laughing loudly. Sue smiled and crossed her wings. She was very pleased with herself. Sean, on the other hand, was crushed. He lowered his head and fell back down in his chair, brooding.

Ms. Goldspeak knitted her brows. She stood quickly, intending to silence them. Before she could open her beak, though, a plump ball of yellow feathers screeched "Stop!" Near tears, Mixed-Up Chuck blurted out "Sean is my friend! He didn't get mad, and he won't do it again. Now stop acting like dumb-dumbs. Can't you see you're hitting his feelings?"

After Ms. Goldspeak gained control of her class again, quieted her students down, corrected Sue, soothed Chuck, and restored the class's focus on the lessons in *Henny Penny*, she recited the following poem:

> Words can hurt & confuse,
> though you may not intend.
> Like the sky that was falling,
> tricked poor Henny Pen.
>
> So say first to yourself,
> to pass the heart test.
> Then say what you mean,
> so we won't have to guess.

Words can hurt & confuse, though you may not intend,
like the sky that was falling, tricked poor Henny Pen.
So say first to yourself, to pass the heart test.
Then say what you mean, so we won't have to guess.

The End

BeakSpeak Character Traits

Can you name some of the character traits that you have observed about the 7 student pullets and cockerels, on pages 1-5, as they talked and faced off in the chicken yard before school? Give an example to support your opinion.

Sue: _____
_____
Renee: _____
_____
Walt: _____
_____
Sean: _____
_____
Jayne: _____
_____
Chuck: _____
_____
Chase: _____
_____

Page 6
Irony means having the opposite of what you expect to happen, happen. How does page five end with two levels of irony: managing time, and defeating bullies?
_____
_____
_____
_____

Lessons

BeakSpeak Lesson Questions

Page 8
1. What are the street-talk words Walt uses?
2. What does he really mean?

Page 9
1. What does Sue say that isn't new?
2. What might she have said in the second part of her sentence that would show what she means in the first part?

Page 10
1. What does Jayne say that suggests groups of chickens are all the same? Do you agree?
2. What might she have said that would allow chickens in the same group to be different?

Page 12
1. What words or sounds does Chase use to fill his speaking pauses?
2. Are they needed? If so, which ones?
3. If there are any, do those add to what he is saying?

Page 14
1. What are the street-talk words Walt uses?
2. How might he have better said what he meant?

Page 15
3. Why does Ms. Goldspeak like Chase to wait before explaining his meaning?
4. Do you think Chase can also talk himself into some courage by waiting?

Lessons

Page 16
1. What does Renee re-say?
2. With what might she replace "that's what she got" to explain *why* she said Henny Penny "got mad at the sky"?
3. What do you think Walt's posture* says about his attitude*?
4. What does Jayne say that tells you she thinks certain chickens are "all the same?"
5. Why do you think she feels this way?
6. Would you agree with her if you were talking about people? Why or why not?
7. Can you think of an example from your own life where this happens with people?
8. What should Jayne have said instead?
9. Since she is her best friend, would Jayne still agree with Renee even if she thought Renee was wrong? Should she?

Page 17
1. Which are the street-talk words Walt uses?
2. What are the proper English words he might have used instead?
3. Since Walt is red, and is angry, is it because he is red?
4. If it's not because he is red, then why is he angry?

Page 19
1. What short cut does Sean use for actual words?
2. How should he have written what he was trying to say instead?
3. Did Sean become upset because he is red? If not, why not?

* posture – the way he sits or stands
* attitude – the way he feels

Lessons

Page 21
1. What are Walt's street-talk words?
2. What does he really mean?
3. What does Sue say that is nothing new?
4. What might she have said that would be closer to her meaning?
5. What does she say to be funny that is actually quite cruel?

Page 22
1. What word gives Mixed-Up Chuck his nick name?
2. What does he actually intend to say?
3. How do you feel about Chuck coming to Sean's rescue?
4. Should Ms. Goldspeak correct Sue privately? In front of Sean only? In front of the whole class?
5. Explain the reasons for your answers.
6. If you were Ms. Goldspeak, what would you say to Chuck in front of the class?
7. Since this story is a fable, what would you say it's moral, or lesson, would be?

BeakSpeak Suggested Answers to Character Traits

1. **Sue:** is a friendly pullet who likes to be in charge of things, like starting the kickball game. Her feelings can be hurt, which Jayne does.
2. **Renee:** likes to make the class laugh, get her teachers attention by waving her wings wildly – even knocking over her desk. She is loyal to her friend, Jayne, even if it means being mean to others.
3. **Walt:** is bossy and likes to make fun of others. He's a bully, but can't stand for others to bully him. He tells Sue he is taking charge of the kickball game, and gets really mad in the classroom when others say his answers about Henny Penny are wrong.
4. **Sean:** has a handicap, a crooked beak, so feels different to others and is unable to speak properly. He makes up for it by isolating himself from other chickens and spending all his time in his electronic world.
5. **Jayne:** is a very aggressive, prejudiced pullet. She attacks Walt for being a bully and holds grudges against chickens who are of a different color to her.
6. **Chuck:** is a very caring cockerel, but gets his words mixed up all the time. He sees a lot of sound-alike words in place of the correct ones, like "you could have stilled him" instead of killed him.
7. **Chase:** is insecure because he's so small. He becomes braver and contributes to class only when an authority figure, like Ms. Goldspeak, is in charge.

<u>Irony involving managing time</u>:

Sue wanted to start a friendly kickball game to pass time before the Headrooster crowed. Instead, they had a heated argument for the entire time. Just when they were ready to truly play, the Headrooster crowed.

<u>Irony involving defeating bullies</u>:

Jayne defeated the bully Walt by bullying him.

BeakSpeak Suggested Lesson Answers

Page 8
1. Good egg
2. That she is a good chicken

Page 9
1. Henny Penny is nice all the time and never gets mean.
2. Henny Penny is nice every time she smiles and greets even strangers with kind words.

Page 10
1. Everybody knows red chickens get mad all the time. No
2. Most chickens get mad sometimes, no matter what color they are.

Page 12
1. Like, like, like, like, uh, like
2. No. None
3. No

Page 14
1. Bad rap, freaked
2. Misunderstood or wrong; became frantic*

Page 15
1. It would help him get his thoughts in order so he wouldn't need to use empty words and sounds.
2. Also, he could find some courage to face Walt.

Page 16
1. Got mad at the sky, that's what she got
2. Got mad at the sky because it fell on her
3. That he feels criticized and angry
4. Red chickens get mad all the time; yellow chickens are always afraid.

---

* frantic – panic-stricken   Answers

5. Either because she saw Walt and Sean get mad earlier in the school yard, or because she's trying to be mean to them, or because she's seen them mad more than she's seen other chickens mad, or because she is biased against red chickens; also, she thinks the color yellow mean cowardly. If that were the case, then Chuck would be a coward.
6. No. Like people, all chickens are different in some way, no matter their color.
7. Some people think red-headed people are quick to anger.
8. That some poultry breeds* seem to have anger problems and some don't
9. If she would, she would be saying loyalty* means more to her than the truth.

Page 17
1. Freak, chills, dude, roasted, cool
2. Grew frantic*; relaxes; cockerel; criticized; likeable or socially admired*
3. No
4. He feels that he, and what he says, is not being respected.

Page 19
1. Ogr8 b4 ne1 thnx he noz my biz plz m8k shr u get enuf fax!
2. O great. Before anyone thinks he knows my business, please make sure you get enough facts!
3. No. He doesn't want to participate in any world but his tech world, and he had his phone taken away, thanks to Walt calling attention to him.

Page 21
1. Kicked you in the pants
2. Who got you riled up*?
3. Beating around the bush, hen-pecked
4. Avoiding what you are really trying to say; lets his wife tell him what to do
5. Your dad is hen-pecked, and your grandpa got crispy-fried at Chicken Lickin.'

* poultry breeds – kinds of different chickens
* loyalty – belief in and faith in someone no matter what
* frantic – panic-stricken
* socially admired – respected by classmates and friends
* riled up – upset

Answers

Page 22

1. Didn't get mad and won't do it again; hitting his feelings
2. If he got mad, he won't do it again; hurting his feelings
3. Good. It's better to be kind than cruel.
4. In private. Then she has to apologize to Sean one-on-one. Then she has to apologize to the whole class.
5. Privately because Sue needs to know what she did was wrong and that Ms. Goldspeak won't allow such a thing in her class. One-on-one to Sean because he's the only one she singled out, and he was deeply hurt. Then apologize to the whole class, too, because she made them a party in hurting and embarrassing Chuck just to make her seem clever*.
6. I would tell him that I was proud of him for going against the whole class to show that he has a good heart and believes in kindness.
7. It's always best to be kind to one another.

* clever – smart

Answers

Teachers: Download document size, printable worksheets, with name and date sections incorporated, for your classrooms at:

www.ErinGoBraghPublishing.com/books/beakspeak

Peggy Marceaux is a retired English teacher who lives in Canyon Lake, Texas. She earned her Bachelor's Degree from Lamar University and her Masters of Arts from the University of Houston, where she specialized in British Literature.

Ms. Marceaux taught for 32 years; 11 in the Alvin Independent School District and 15 in the Comal Independent School District in TX, Chairing the High School English Departments in both.

Having raised chickens for twenty years, she loved the diversity among the breeds. This inspired "BeakSpeak", a story designed to help young people accept their differences and build confidence, through speech validation. Ever the English teacher, Ms. Marceaux believes the earlier you teach children language precision, the better it will help them succeed in their future relationships and careers.

CPSIA information can be obtained
at www.ICGtesting.com
Printed in the USA
LVHW050259060919
629980LV00002B/5/P